In an
Average
Lifetime...

IN AN AVERAGE LIFETIME...

TOM HEYMANN

FAWCETT COLUMBINE • NEW YORK

A Fawcett Columbine Book
Published by Ballantine Books

Library of Congress Catalog Card Number: 90-85059
ISBN: 0-449-90544-6

Cover design by Dale Fiorillo
Text design by Beth Tondreau Design / Mary A. Wirth

Manufactured in the United States of America

First Edition: January 1992
10 9 8 7 6 5 4 3 2 1

To my family
and our, more or less,
"average lifetimes" together.

ACKNOWLEDGMENTS

I want to thank my friends, and literary agents, Herbert and Nancy Katz. Also, to my editor, Elisa Wares, for her continuing enthusiasm.

AUTHOR'S NOTE

Several assumptions had to be made in order to create this book. First of all, presented within this book is a profile of the "average American." While we all know that the average American has not yet been born, other than in statistical portraits and demographic profiles, this hypothetical person does allow us to view an embodiment of the idiosyncrasies of all Americans, including ourselves.

Second, the statistics in this book reflect today's population, usage of time, and consumption of goods. Consequently, no allowance has been made for trends that may or may not occur in the future. Monetary figures are based on today's dollar, while a lifetime is based on the current average expected lifespan of 74.9 years.

Third, the information sources cited in this book provided the basic raw data upon which the book's statistics are based. In a very few instances, the sources did provide data in terms of a person's lifetime.

While there has been substantial growth in the demographic interest in lifetime statistics, *In An Average Lifetime* represents the first known effort to present a comprehensive statistical portrait of the lifetime of the average American.

INTRODUCTION

The average American lives to be 74.9 years of age. That gives each of us 899 months; 27,339 days; 656,136 hours; or 39,368,160 minutes to sleep, eat, work, play, or otherwise pass the time. During our lives we experience and engage in a broad range of activities—from wearing diapers to opening junk mail, from cleaning our homes to paying taxes. At first, it may not seem significant that we spend a certain amount of time each day engaged in a specific pursuit. When we look at our chosen activities over the course of our lifetimes, however, they begin to take on a different magnitude, that of an investment.

We can learn a great deal about ourselves by examining our usage of time and our consumption of resources. We can determine whether we are more devoted to our careers or to our families; whether we would rather sleep or spend more time in waking activities; whether we would rather have sex or watch television. All of our priorities become very apparent when we look at ourselves in terms of a lifetime of choices.

In An Average Lifetime is an attempt to put our lives into perspective. It allows each American to consider his or her life and gives each of us the opportunity to make adjustments in light of this information. At the very least, this book will give us reason for pause when we are sitting in afternoon traffic, attending a lengthy business meeting, eating another bag of potato chips, or watching television. It's your life. Spend it as you wish. You have just used approximately one minute of it reading this introduction.

IN AN
AVERAGE
LIFETIME...

IN AN AVERAGE LIFETIME...

... the average American celebrates 74 birthdays

IN AN AVERAGE LIFETIME...

... the average American receives 333 birthday presents

IN AN AVERAGE LIFETIME...

... the average American receives 2,322
greeting cards

Of those,

... 524 are birthday cards

IN AN AVERAGE LIFETIME...

... the average American "rings in" 74
new years

IN AN AVERAGE LIFETIME...

... the average American is counted in 7 censuses

IN AN AVERAGE LIFETIME...

... the average American files 42 income tax returns

... the average American spends 464 hours preparing his or her income tax returns

IN AN AVERAGE LiFETiME...

... the average American earns $1,235,720
Of that,
... $178,364 is paid in taxes

IN AN AVERAGE LiFETiME...

... the average American man is in the work force for 38 years, 9 months, and 18 days

... the average American woman is in the work force for 29 years, 4 months, and 24 days

IN AN AVERAGE LifETiME...

... the average American man holds 4 jobs

... the average American woman holds
6 jobs

IN AN AVERAGE LiFETiME...

... the average American spends 70,696 hours working

Of that time,

... he or she spends 24,305 hours earning enough money to pay taxes

... he or she spends 22,623 hours "goofing off"

IN AN AVERAGE LIFETIME...

... the average American spends 3 years in business meetings

IN AN AVERAGE LiFETiME...

... the average American spends 10
months commuting to and from work

IN AN AVERAGE LIFETIME...

... the average American takes 12 adult-education classes

Of those,

... 8 are job related

... 3 are for personal or social satisfaction

... 1 is for general education

IN AN AVERAGE LIFETIME...

... the average American spends 12 years and 8 months in school

... the average American spends 13 years and 4 months watching television

Of that time spent watching television,

... 2 years and 7 months is spent watching commercials

IN AN AVERAGE LIFETIME...

... the average American, while watching television, changes the channel 325,393 times

IN AN AVERAGE LIFETIME...

... the average American spends the equivalent of 3,417 days listening to the radio

Of that time,

... 550 days are spent listening to commercials

IN AN AVERAGE LIFETIME...

... the average American spends the equivalent of 30 months reading newspapers

Of that time,

... 6 months are spent looking at advertisements

IN AN AVERAGE LIFETIME...

... the average American is hit with
136,692,500 advertisements and
commercial messages

Of those,

... 18,549,172 are noticed

... 2,925,220 are remembered

IN AN AVERAGE LIFETIME...

... the average American is the target of advertisements from a variety of media, including

... 15,309,560 from newspapers

... 12,220,310 from magazines

... 5,905,116 from billboards

... 1,749,664 from television

... 1,448,941 from radio

IN AN AVERAGE LIFETIME...

... advertisers spend $35,943 trying to influence the average American

Of that,

... $9,499 is spent in newspapers

... $7,821 is spent on television

... $6,455 is spent on direct mail

... $2,374 is spent on radio

... $2,369 is spent on Yellow Pages

... $1,849 is spent in magazines

... $324 is spent on billboards

IN AN AVERAGE LiFETiME...

... the average American receives 49,060 pieces of mail

Of those,

... 18,187 are pieces of direct-mail advertising

Of those,

... 8,002 are never opened

IN AN AVERAGE LIFETIME...

... the average American receives quantities of junk mail from the following groups:

... 7,457 pieces from department stores

... 6,365 pieces from magazines

... 1,819 pieces from credit card companies

... 1,455 pieces from contest companies

... 364 pieces from supermarkets

... 364 pieces from religious organizations

... 363 pieces from political groups and politicians

IN AN AVERAGE LIFETIME...

... direct-mail advertisers destroy 112 trees sending 1,218 pounds of junk mail to the average American

... the average American spends the equivalent of 8 months opening junk mail

IN AN AVERAGE LIFETIME...

... the average American buys 86
magazine subscriptions

IN AN AVERAGE LIFETIME...

... the average American reads 8,988 magazines

Over the course of

... the equivalent of 285 days

IN AN AVERAGE LIFETIME...

... the average American spends $10,636 on reading materials

Of that,

... $5,070 is spent on books

IN AN AVERAGE LIFETIME...

... the average American buys 668 books
   Of those,
... 248 are hardcover
... 420 are softcover

IN AN AVERAGE LIFETIME...

... the average American borrows 374
items (books, tapes, etc.) from libraries

IN AN AVERAGE LIFETIME...

... the average American spends 10,935 hours reading

... the average American spends 117,048 hours watching television

IN AN AVERAGE LifETiME...

... the average American spends 117 hours in museums

... the average American spends 1,091 hours in movie theaters

IN AN AVERAGE LIFETIME...

... the average American attends

... 7 symphony concerts

... 5 operas

... 2 Broadway shows

IN AN AVERAGE LIFETIME...

... the average American attends
... 16 major league baseball games
... 11 professional football games
... 4 professional basketball games
... 4 professional hockey games

IN AN AVERAGE LIFETIME...

... the average American visits 31 animal parks

Of those visits,

... 21 are to zoos and wildlife parks

... 10 are to aquariums and marine wildlife attractions

IN AN AVERAGE LifETimE...

... the average American visits 48 fairs and expositions

IN AN AVERAGE LIFETIME...

... the average American spends 360 hours visiting 72 amusement parks and attractions

IN AN AVERAGE LIFETIME...

... the average American spends 2,280 hours visiting 86 federal recreation areas

Including

... 17 national parks

... 7 national historical parks

... 7 national monuments

IN AN AVERAGE LIFETIME...

... the average American spends 19 nights camping

IN AN AVERAGE LiFETiME...

... the average American attends 35
weddings

IN AN AVERAGE LIFETIME...

... the average American goes bowling 233 times

IN AN AVERAGE LIFETIME...

... the average American sees

... 345 movies in theaters

... 630 movies on videocassettes

IN AN AVERAGE LiFETiME...

... the average American purchases 232 records, tapes, CDs, etc.

IN AN AVERAGE LIFETIME...

... the average American makes 184,702 phone calls

Of those,

... 166,699 are local

... 17,827 are long distance

... 176 are overseas

IN AN AVERAGE LIFETIME...

... the average American spends the equivalent of 2½ years speaking

... the average American spends the equivalent of 2 years on the telephone

IN AN AVERAGE LiFETiME...

... the average American receives 31
prank phone calls

IN AN AVERAGE LIFETIME...

... the average American is interviewed by public opinion research organizations 18 times

... the average American spends 9 hours responding to public opinion surveys

IN AN AVERAGE LIFETIME...

... the average American's household is touched by 19 crimes of violence or theft

Of those crimes,

... 4 are violent (rape, robbery, or assault)

IN AN AVERAGE LIFETIME...

... the average American loses $980 to
robbers and burglars

IN AN AVERAGE LIFETIME...

... the average American spends 17,307 hours eating meals at home

... the average American spends 16,961 hours preparing those meals and cleaning up

IN AN AVERAGE LIFETIME...

... the average American spends $89,281 on food

Of that,

... $56,520 is spent eating at home

... $32,761 is spent eating out

IN AN AVERAGE LIFETIME...

... the average American eats out at restaurants 14,411 times

Including

... 1,811 trips to McDonald's

IN AN AVERAGE LIFETIME...

... the average American spends 8,657
hours eating out at restaurants

IN AN AVERAGE LIFETIME...

... the average American spends $66,632 on packaged food products

Of that money,

... $6,057 goes toward the cost of the products' packaging

IN AN AVERAGE LIFETIME...

... the average American spends $6,881 in vending machines

IN AN AVERAGE LIFETIME...

... the average American spends
... $1,331 on home-delivered foods
... $23,547 on alcoholic beverages

IN AN AVERAGE LIFETIME...

... the average American consumes 10,231 gallons of beverages

IN AN AVERAGE LiFETiME...

... the average American drinks 115 gallons of liquor

Including

... 46 gallons of whiskey

... 25 gallons of vodka

... 11 gallons of gin

... 9 gallons of cordials

IN AN AVERAGE LIFETIME...

... the average American drinks 20,301
bottles of beer

IN AN AVERAGE LIFETIME...

... the average American drinks 1,019 glasses of wine

IN AN AVERAGE LIFETIME...

... the average American drinks 23 glasses of champagne

IN AN AVERAGE LIFETIME...

... the average American drinks 6,220 glasses of fruit juice

Including

... 2,583 glasses of orange

... 785 glasses of apple

... 288 glasses of cranberry

... 216 glasses of grape

... 186 glasses of grapefruit

... 66 glasses of pineapple

... 54 glasses of prune

IN AN AVERAGE LIFETIME...

... the average American consumes 56,044 cups of coffee

Including

... 9,295 cups of instant

... 10,389 cups of decaffeinated

... 36,360 of regular

IN AN AVERAGE LiFETIME...

... the average American drinks 15,579 glasses of milk

... the average American drinks 18,995 glasses of soda

IN AN AVERAGE LIFETIME...

... the average American consumes
109,354 pounds of food

IN AN AVERAGE LIFETIME...

... the average American eats 18,276 eggs
Of those,

... 6,214 are eaten scrambled

... 5,666 are eaten fried

... 4,203 are eaten boiled

... 731 are eaten in omelets

... 548 are eaten poached

IN AN AVERAGE LIFETIME...

... the average American eats 18,216
bowls of cereal

IN AN AVERAGE LIFETIME...

... the average American eats 84,775 crackers

Of those,

... 31,386 are salt

... 21,140 are sweet, graham

... 12,727 are cheese flavor

IN AN AVERAGE LIFETIME...

... the average American eats 1,798 pounds of cheese

Including

... 794 pounds of cheddar

... 419 pounds of mozzarella

... 135 pounds of American

... 90 pounds of Swiss

IN AN AVERAGE LiFETiME...

... the average American eats 8,621
   pounds of red meat
   Including
... 5,108 pounds of beef
... 3,348 pounds of pork
... 82 pounds of veal
... 75 pounds of lamb and mutton

IN AN AVERAGE LIFETIME...

... the average American eats 4,277
   pounds of poultry
   Including
... 3,333 pounds of chicken
... 944 pounds of turkey

IN AN AVERAGE LIFETIME...

... the average American eats 1,124 pounds of fish

Including

... 270 pounds of canned tuna

IN AN AVERAGE LiFETiME...

... the average American eats 5,842 bowls of pasta

IN AN AVERAGE LIFETIME...

... the average American eats 6,991 hot dogs

... the average American eats 8,389 hamburgers

IN AN AVERAGE LiFETiME...

... the average American consumes 232 pounds of spices

Including

... 79 pounds of mustard seed

... 37 pounds of sesame seed

... 35 pounds of pepper

... 10 pounds of dried chili peppers

IN AN AVERAGE LIFETIME...

... the average American eats 7,460 pounds of fresh vegetables

Including

... 1,790 pounds of lettuce

... 891 pounds of onions and shallots

... 839 pounds of tomatoes

... 569 pounds of cabbage

... 532 pounds of celery

... 517 pounds of carrots

... 487 pounds of corn

... 307 pounds of cucumbers

IN AN AVERAGE LiFETiME...

... the average American eats 7,071
   pounds of fresh fruit
   Including
... 1,813 pounds of bananas
... 1,431 pounds of apples
... 1,086 pounds of oranges
... 502 pounds of grapes
... 487 pounds of grapefruit
... 360 pounds of peaches
... 240 pounds of strawberries
... 217 pounds of pears

IN AN AVERAGE LIFETIME...

... the average American eats 8,284 apples
Including

... 3,396 Red Delicious

... 1,408 Golden Delicious

... 580 McIntosh

... 529 Rome

... 456 Granny Smith

... 316 Jonathan

IN AN AVERAGE LIFETIME...

... the average American eats 152 pies
Of those,
... 114 are apple pies

IN AN AVERAGE LIFETIME...

... the average American eats 35,138 cookies

Of those,

... 10,532 are sandwich-style

... 4,573 are chocolate chip

IN AN AVERAGE LIFETIME...

... the average American eats 609
brownies

IN AN AVERAGE LIFETIME...

... the average American eats 269 gallons of ice cream

Including

... 78 gallons of vanilla

... 24 gallons of chocolate

... 14 gallons of strawberry

IN AN AVERAGE LIFETIME...

... the average American eats 1,483
pounds of candy

Including

... 801 pounds of chocolate

IN AN AVERAGE LIFETIME...

... the average American eats 1,279 pounds of snack food

Including

... 443 pounds of potato chips

... 248 pounds of tortilla chips

... 85 pounds of pretzels

... 67 pounds of corn chips

... 4 pounds of pork rinds

IN AN AVERAGE LIFETIME...

... the average American eats 512 pounds
of peanuts

Of that,

... 250 pounds are eaten in peanut butter

... 98 pounds are eaten in candy

IN AN AVERAGE LIFETIME...

... the average American eats 4,194 quarts of popcorn

Of that,

... 2,936 quarts are eaten at home

... 1,258 quarts are eaten at theaters, stadiums, etc.

IN AN AVERAGE LiFETiME...

... the average American spends $408 on vitamins

... the average American spends $1,157 on potato chips

IN AN AVERAGE LIFETIME...

... the average American spends

... $3,806 on diet food

... $19,791 on fast-food

IN AN AVERAGE LIFETIME...

... the average American suffers 223
attacks of heartburn

IN AN AVERAGE LIFETIME...

... the average American eats 304 Dunkin'
Donuts

Of those,

... 152 are eaten for breakfast

IN AN AVERAGE LiFETiME...

... the average American eats 240
Hershey's Kisses

IN AN AVERAGE LifETimE...

... the average American eats 1,889
Tootsie Rolls

IN AN AVERAGE LIFETIME...

... the average American eats 11,113 M&M's

Of those,

... 3,334 are brown

... 2,223 are red

... 2,223 are yellow

... 2,222 are green or tan*

... 1,111 are orange

*tan is used only in regular (not peanut) M&M's

IN AN AVERAGE LiFETiME...

... the average American consumes 4,659 pounds of sugar

IN AN AVERAGE LIFETIME...

... the average American visits the dentist 142 times

IN AN AVERAGE LIFETIME...

... the average American has his or her teeth cleaned 41 times

IN AN AVERAGE LIFETIME...

... the average American has 60 cavities filled

IN AN AVERAGE LIFETIME...

... the average American has 11 teeth extracted

IN AN AVERAGE LIFETIME...

... the average American gets the flu 17
times

IN AN AVERAGE LIFETIME...

... the average American takes 8,891
aspirin tablets

IN AN AVERAGE LiFETiME...

... the average American visits the doctor 194 times

Of those visits,

... 59 are to a general or family practitioner

... 23 are to an internist

... 22 are to a pediatrician

... 12 are to an ophthalmologist

... 5 are to a psychiatrist

IN AN AVERAGE LIFETIME...

... the average American spends 49 hours seeing doctors

... the average American spends 64 hours waiting to see doctors

IN AN AVERAGE LIFETIME...

... the average American has 10 rectal exams

IN AN AVERAGE LIFETIME...

... the average American has 12 vision tests

IN AN AVERAGE LIFETIME...

... the average American has 17 X rays
   Of those,
... 5 are chest X rays
... 3 are unnecessary

IN AN AVERAGE LIFETIME...

... the average American has urinalysis
performed 27 times

IN AN AVERAGE LIFETIME...

... the average American has 31 blood tests

IN AN AVERAGE LifETIME...

... the average American has his or her
blood pressure checked 75 times

IN AN AVERAGE LIFETIME...

... the average American has 463 prescriptions filled

At a cost of

... $7,692

IN AN AVERAGE LifETiME...

... the average American is injured 19 times

Of those injuries,

... 6 occur in the home

IN AN AVERAGE LIFETIME...

... the average American is involved in 6 motor vehicle accidents

In which

... he or she is injured twice

IN AN AVERAGE LifETiME...

... the average American man is
hospitalized 8 times

... the average American woman is
hospitalized 12 times

IN AN AVERAGE LIFETIME...

... the average American man spends 58 days in the hospital

... the average American woman spends 72 days in the hospital

IN AN AVERAGE LIFETIME...

... the average American spends 69 years and 11 months indoors

... the average American spends 5 years outdoors

IN AN AVERAGE LIFETIME...

... the average American spends 5 years
waiting in lines

IN AN AVERAGE LIFETIME...

... the average American spends 7 years
in the bathroom

IN AN AVERAGE LIFETIME...

... the average American spends 1 year
and 4 months washing and grooming

... the average American spends 1 year
and 6 months getting dressed

IN AN AVERAGE LIFETIME...

... the average American woman weighs herself 8,491 times

... the average American man weighs himself 9,815 times

IN AN AVERAGE LIFETIME...

... the average American takes 25,972 showers

Lasting a total of

... 126 days

IN AN AVERAGE LIFETIME...

... the average American woman washes her hair 15,696 times

... the average American man washes his hair 18,325 times

IN AN AVERAGE LIFETIME...

... the average American spends 911 hours brushing his/her teeth

IN AN AVERAGE LIFETIME...

... the average American uses 9,662 yards (nearly 6 miles) of dental floss

IN AN AVERAGE LiFETiME...

... the average American purchases 100
    toothbrushes

IN AN AVERAGE LIFETIME...

... each of the average American's toenails grows 19.5 inches

IN AN AVERAGE LIFETIME...

... each of the average American's fingernails grows 77.9 inches

IN AN AVERAGE LiFETiME...

... each of the average American man's whiskers grows 27.5 feet

IN AN AVERAGE LIFETIME...

... each of the average American's hairs grows 40 feet and 7 inches

IN AN AVERAGE LIFETIME...

... the average American has 664 haircuts

IN AN AVERAGE LiFETiME...

... the average American breathes
551,144,160 times

Taking in

... 68,893,020 gallons of air

IN AN AVERAGE LiFETiME...

... the average American smoker consumes 590,105 cigarettes (29,505 packs)

While

... the average American nonsmoker inhales the equivalent of 13,669 cigarettes (683 packs)

IN AN AVERAGE LIFETIME...

... the average American's heart pumps
2,755,720,800 times

Circulating

... 55,000,000 gallons of blood

IN AN AVERAGE LIFETIME...

... the average American blinks
393,674,400 times

Causing his/her eyes to be shut for

... 1 1/2 years

IN AN AVERAGE LIFETIME...

... the average American grows 899 new layers of skin

IN AN AVERAGE LifETiME...

... the average American spends 3,893 hours playing active sports

... the average American loses 5,126 gallons of perspiration

IN AN AVERAGE LIFETIME...

... the average American spends 957 days shopping

Including

... 478 days buying groceries, clothing, and other basics

... 115 days visiting hair salons, post offices, banks, and other services

... 48 days shopping for cars, furniture, or houses

IN AN AVERAGE LIFETIME...

... the average American spends 9 months traveling to and from stores

IN AN AVERAGE LiFETIME...

... the average American deposits $700 into parking meters

IN AN AVERAGE LIFETIME...

... the average American receives 3,775 catalogs through the mail

... the average American spends $9,439 buying products through catalogs

IN AN AVERAGE LIFETIME...

... the average American man visits a shopping mall 37 times

... the average American woman visits a shopping mall 66 times

IN AN AVERAGE LiFETiME...

... the average American man spends
$1,554 in shopping malls

... the average American woman spends
$3,234 in shopping malls

IN AN AVERAGE LiFETiME...

... the average American acquires five
credit cards

... the average American carries an
average balance of $1,661 in credit-
card debt

IN AN AVERAGE LIFETIME...

... the average American makes 1,655
credit-card purchases

Charging
... $120,875

IN AN AVERAGE LIFETIME...

... the average American uses an
   automated teller machine 1,492 times
   Withdrawing a total of
... $38,059

IN AN AVERAGE LIFETIME...

... the average American writes 15,224
checks

Of those,

... 152 "bounce"

IN AN AVERAGE LIFETIME...

... the average American makes 8,958 trips to the supermarket

Spending

... $288,215

IN AN AVERAGE LIFETIME...

... the average American receives 67,288 manufacturer's discount coupons with a value of $25,576

Of those,

... the average American redeems 2,131 coupons worth $822

IN AN AVERAGE LIFETIME...

... the average American spends
... $35 on sleeping pills
... $3,342 on coffee

IN AN AVERAGE LIFETIME...

... the average American spends
... $20 on drainpipe openers
... $152 on laxatives

IN AN AVERAGE LIFETIME...

... the average American spends $79 on potpourri

... the average American woman wears $1,583 worth of perfume

IN AN AVERAGE LIFETIME...

... the average American man spends
$27,972 on clothes

... the average American woman spends
$38,228 on clothes

IN AN AVERAGE LIFETIME...

... the average American buys 121 pairs
of jeans

... the average American buys 494 T-shirts

IN AN AVERAGE LIFETIME...

... the average American man buys 510 pairs of hosiery

... the average American woman buys 1,264 pairs of hosiery

Of those,

... 899 pairs are panty hose

IN AN AVERAGE LIFETIME...

... the average American buys 292 pairs of shoes

Of those,

... 112 pairs are sneakers

IN AN AVERAGE LIFETIME...

... the average American woman buys 22 bathing suits

IN AN AVERAGE LIFETIME...

... the average American buys 31 pairs of sunglasses

IN AN AVERAGE LIFETIME...

... the average American buys 6 cameras

IN AN AVERAGE LIFETIME...

... the average American takes 4,613 photographs

Of those,

... 4,059 are taken in color

... 554 are taken in black and white

... 132 are taken at Disney parks (Disneyland, etc.)

IN AN AVERAGE LIFETIME...

...the average American buys

...7 color televisions

...8 radios

...9 telephones

IN AN AVERAGE LIFETIME...

... the average American spends $3,730 on lottery tickets

... the average American wins $1,825 playing the lottery

IN AN AVERAGE LIFETIME...

... the average American buys 47 boxes of
Girl Scout cookies

IN AN AVERAGE LIFETIME...

... the average American donates $26,398 to charities

... the average American spends $48,259 on toys

IN AN AVERAGE LIFETIME...

... the average American buys 11 board games

Of those,

... 6 are children's games

... 5 are family or adult games

IN AN AVERAGE LifETIME...

... the average American buys
... 18 puzzles
... 32 stuffed animals
... 48 dolls

IN AN AVERAGE LIFETIME...

... the average American buys 609
Crayola crayons

IN AN AVERAGE LIFETIME...

... the average American spends $19,292 buying gifts

Of that,

... $9,651 is spent on Christmas presents

IN AN AVERAGE LIFETIME...

... the average American purchases 1,049 flowers

Of those,

... 262 are roses

... 199 are given on birthdays

... 157 are given on Valentine's Days

... 136 are given on Mother's Days

IN AN AVERAGE LIFETIME...

... the average American takes 269 vacations

Of those,

... 130 are weekend trips

IN AN AVERAGE LIFETIME...

... the average American takes 42,481 automobile trips

Of those,

... 13,093 are work-related

... 8,491 are taken for shopping

... 4,202 are taken visiting friends

... 515 are taken to the doctor or dentist

... 143 are taken for pleasure

... 57 are taken for vacations

IN AN AVERAGE LIFETIME...

... the average American drives 413,226 miles

Including

... 141,737 miles driven to and from work

... 56,199 miles driven to visit friends or relatives

... 55,372 miles driven on shopping trips

... 8,678 miles driven on vacations

... 6,198 miles driven to the doctor or dentist

... 4,132 miles driven for sheer pleasure

IN AN AVERAGE LIFETIME...

... the average American owns five cars
   Of those,
... at least one will be recalled for
   manufacturing defects

IN AN AVERAGE LIFETIME...

... the average American washes his/her car 459 times

IN AN AVERAGE LIFETIME...

... the average American,

... cannot start his/her car 14 times

... needs to have his/her car towed 8 times

... has 3 flat tires

... is locked out of his/her car twice

IN AN AVERAGE LIFETIME...

... the average American purchases 4
bicycles

IN AN AVERAGE LIFETIME...

... the average American walks 92,375 miles

IN AN AVERAGE LIFETIME...

... the average American travels 622,736 miles in motorized vehicles

Including

... 482,892 miles in cars

... 128,883 miles in airplanes

... 7,003 miles in buses

... 3,958 miles in trains

IN AN AVERAGE LIFETIME...

... the average American takes 139 plane trips

Including

... 128 domestic flights

... 11 international flights

IN AN AVERAGE LIFETIME...

... of the average American's 139 plane
   trips,

... 115 take off on time

... 106 arrive on time

IN AN AVERAGE LiFETiME...

... the average American spends 4 years traveling in automobiles

Of that time,

... 6 months is spent waiting for red lights to turn green

IN AN AVERAGE LIFETIME...

... the average American wastes approximately 9 months sitting in traffic congestion

IN AN AVERAGE LiFETiME...

... the average American uses 21,553 gallons of gasoline

Of that,

... 1,078 gallons are wasted while sitting in traffic

IN AN AVERAGE LIFETIME...

... the average American uses (for other than drinking purposes) 2,733,850 gallons of water

Of that,

... 1,093,540 gallons are used while flushing the toilet

... 546,770 gallons are used taking showers and baths

... 410,078 gallons are used in the bathroom sink

... 328,062 gallons are used doing laundry

... 273,385 gallons are used in the kitchen

... 82,015 gallons are used outside

IN AN AVERAGE LIFETIME...

... the average American uses

... 10,370 aluminum cans

... 12,788 glass bottles and jars

... 48,715 pounds of paper products

IN AN AVERAGE LIFETIME...

... the average American produces 95,685 pounds of garbage

Of that,

... 76,548 pounds are sent to landfills

... 10,525 pounds are recycled

... 5,741 pounds are converted to energy

... 2,871 pounds are incinerated

IN AN AVERAGE LIFETIME...

... the average American's trash includes

... 16,908 pounds of yard waste

... 14,812 pounds of food waste

... 11,023 pounds of durable goods

... 9,406 pounds of cardboard

... 9,004 pounds of mixed paper

... 7,023 pounds of newspaper

... 4,583 pounds of books and magazines

... 4,268 pounds of beer and soft drink bottles

IN AN AVERAGE LIFETIME...

... the average American throws out

... 67 tires

... 487 pens

... 609 razors

... 5,480 disposable diapers

IN AN AVERAGE LIFETIME...

... the average American buys 913 disposable batteries

Of those,

... 177 are used in toys and games

... 172 are used in tape recorders

... 132 are used in flashlights and lanterns

... 96 are used in cameras

... 90 are used in radios

... 51 are used in clocks

... 33 are used in calculators

... 27 are used in smoke detectors

IN AN AVERAGE LIFETIME...

... the average American uses 14,231 pounds of plastic

Of that,

... 4,494 pounds are product packaging which is discarded as soon as the package is opened

IN AN AVERAGE LIFETIME...

... the average American wears 7,500 diapers

IN AN AVERAGE LifETiME...

... the average American opens the refrigerator 231,323 times

IN AN AVERAGE LIFETIME...

... the average American moves 14 times
Of those moves,
... 9 are within the same county
... 3 are within the same state
... 2 are to a different state

IN AN AVERAGE LifETiME...

... the average American spends $30,787 on home improvements

IN AN AVERAGE LifETiME...

... the average American rearranges his or her furniture 177 times

IN AN AVERAGE LIFETIME...

... the average American spends 9,346 hours cleaning his/her house

... the average American spends 3,084 hours thinking or just relaxing

IN AN AVERAGE LIFETIME...

... the average American washes 8,493 loads of laundry

Containing

... 127,395 items of clothing

IN AN AVERAGE LIFETIME...

... the average American spends 1 year
looking for misplaced items

IN AN AVERAGE LIFETIME...

... the average American spends 24 years
sleeping

IN AN AVERAGE LIFETIME...

... the average American has 1,947
nightmares

IN AN AVERAGE LiFETiME...

... the average American woman has
83,074 sexual fantasies

IN AN AVERAGE LIFETIME...

... the average American man has 166,148 sexual fantasies

IN AN AVERAGE LIFETIME...

... the average American "falls in love" 6 times

IN AN AVERAGE LIFETIME...

... the average American woman has 3 sex
partners

... the average American man has 12 sex
partners

IN AN AVERAGE LIFETIME...

... the average American woman has sexual intercourse 2,879 times

... the average American man has sexual intercourse 3,778 times

IN AN AVERAGE LIFETIME...

... the average American has 4,438 orgasms

IN AN AVERAGE LIFETIME...

... the average American man cries 1,258 times

... the average American woman cries 4,764 times

IN AN AVERAGE LIFETIME...

... the average American man spends 126 hours crying

... the average American woman spends 476 hours crying

IN AN AVERAGE LIFETIME...

... the average American laughs 410,078
times

SOURCES

AND

INDEX

SOURCES

PAGE
3. Bureau of the Census
4. *On An Average Day* . . .
5. Greeting Card Association
6. Bureau of the Census
7. Same
8. Statistical Abstract
   U.S. News & World Report
9. Department of Labor, Consumer Expenditure
   Survey
   The Tax Foundation
10. Statistical Abstract
11. Same
12. *American Demographics*
    The Tax Foundation
13. *USA Today* (citing Fortino & Associates)
14. *American Demographics*
15. Statistical Abstract
16. Statistical Abstract
    A.C. Nielsen
    Advertising Research Foundation
17. A.C. Nielsen
    USA Today
18. Radio Advertising Bureau
19. Editor & Publisher
20. *American Demographics*
    Marketing News
21. Advertising Research Foundation
22. Statistical Abstract

SOURCES

PAGE

23. U.S. Postal Service
    Direct Marketing Association
    "Earth Day, 1990"
24. Newspaper Advertising Bureau
25. "Earth Day, 1990"
    U.S. News & World Report
26. *The New York Times*
27. National Association of Broadcasters
    Magazine Publishers of America
28. Statistical Abstract
29. Same
30. University of Illinois, Panel on Library Circulation
31. *American Demographics*
    A.C. Nielsen
32. Survey Research Center, University of Maryland
33. Statistical Abstract
34. Same
35. *American Demographics*
36. *USA Today* (citing the International Association of Fairs and Expositions)
37. International Association of Parks and Attractions
    U.S. News & World Report
38. Statistical Abstract
39. National Sporting Goods Association
40. Bureau of the Census
    Bride's Magazine
41. American Bowling Congress

SOURCES

PAGE

42. Motion Picture Association of America, Inc.
    Video Store
43. Statistical Abstract
44. Same
45. *Aeroflot Illustrated Review*
    The New York Times
46. *The New York Times*
47. Walker Research
48. Bureau of Justice Statistics
49. Insurance Information Institute
50. Survey Research Center, University of Maryland
51. Department of Labor, Consumer Expenditure
    Survey
    Department of Agriculture
52. National Restaurant Association
53. Survey Research Center, University of Maryland
54. Department of Labor, Consumer Expenditure
    Survey
    Environmentalizing
55. *The New York Times*
56. Department of Labor, Consumer Expenditure
    Survey
    Department of Agriculture
57. Department of Agriculture
58. *Business Week*
59. Department of Agriculture
60. Same
61. Champagne News and Information Bureau

SOURCES

PAGE

62. Department of Agriculture
63. Department of Agriculture
    USA Today (citing the National Coffee Association)
64. Department of Agriculture
65. Same
66. American Egg Board
    USA Today (citing MRCA Information Services)
67. Department of Agriculture
68. *U.S. News & World Report*
69. Department of Agriculture
70. Same
71. Same
72. Same
73. National Pasta Association
74. American Meat Institute
75. *The New York Times*
    Department of Agriculture
76. Department of Agriculture
77. Same
78. International Apple Institute
79. Same
80. *U.S. News & World Report*
81. *The New York Times*
82. International Ice Cream Association
83. National Confectioners Association
84. Snack Food Association
85. Department of Agriculture
86. The Popcorn Institute

SOURCES

PAGE

87. *On An Average Day . . .*

88. *The New York Times*

89. Glaxo, Inc.

90. *Adweek's Marketing Week*

91. Dunkin' Donuts
    American Health

92. Tootsie Roll Industries

93. M&M/Mars

94. Department of Agriculture

95. National Center for Health Statistics

96. American Dental Association

97. Same

98. Same

99. Statistical Abstract

100. *U.S. News & World Report*

101. *Newsweek*

102. *On An Average Day . . .*

103. National Center for Health Statistics

104. *Wall Street Journal*
     USA Today

105. National Center for Health Statistics

106. Same

107. Same
     Journal of the American Medical Association

108. National Center for Health Statistics

109. Same

110. Same

111. American Pharmaceutical Association

SOURCES

PAGE
112. Statistical Abstract
113. Same
114. Same
115. Same
116. Environmental Protection Agency (EPA)
117. *U.S. News & World Report*
118. *Newsweek* (citing Fortino & Associates)
119. Survey Research Center, University of Maryland
120. *USA Today*
121. Environmental Protection Agency
122. *USA Today* (citing R.H. Bruskin Associates)
123. John O. Butler Company
124. Same
125. Same
126. *U.S. News & World Report*
127. Same
128. *USA Today*
129. *U.S. News & World Report*
130. Reno's International Hair Stylists (Michael Severino, White Plains, NY)
131. *National Geographic*
132. Phillip Morris
     U.S. Department of Health
133. *National Geographic*
134. Same
135. Same
136. Same
137. Survey Research Center, University of Maryland

SOURCES

PAGE

138. Same
139. *USA Today*
140. Direct Marketing Association
    Wall Street Journal
141. *U.S. News & World Report*
142. Same
143. Statistical Abstract
144. *The New York Times*
    Statistical Abstract
145. *The New York Times*
    USA Today
146. *USA Today*
147. Same
148. Same
149. *Adweek's Marketing Week*
    U.S. News & World Report
150. *Adweek's Marketing Week*
    On An Average Day . . .
151. *The New York Times*
152. Department of Labor, Consumer Expenditure Survey
153. *The New York Times*
    USA Today
154. National Association of Hosiery Manufacturers
155. National Shoe Retailers Association
156. *The New York Times*
157. *USA Today*
158. *On An Average Day* . . .
159. Same

SOURCES

PAGE

160. Electronic Industries Association
161. *On An Average Day ...*
162. Girl Scouts of the U.S.A.
163. Statistical Abstract
     On An Average Day ...
164. *Playthings*
165. Same
166. *USA Today*
167. Department of Labor, Consumer Expenditure Survey
     USA Today
168. Society of American Florists
169. U.S. Travel Data Center
170. Department of Transportation
171. Motor Vehicle Manufacturers Association (MVMA)
172. Same
173. International Car Wash Association
174. Automobile Association of America
     MVMA
175. *Bicycling*
176. *Walking*
177. Statistical Abstract
178. Department of Transportation
179. Same
180. Survey Research Center, University of Maryland
     The New York Times
181. The Road Information Program
182. MVMA
     National Wildlife Federation

SOURCES

PAGE

183. National Wildlife Federation
184. *On An Average Day ...*
185. *The New York Times*
186. Same
187. World Wildlife Fund
188. *U.S. News & World Report*
189. *Environmentalizing*
190. *American Health*
191. *Home Energy*
192. Statistical Abstract
193. Bureau of the Census
194. *Spiegel's Home Fashion Monitor*
195. Survey Research Center, University of Maryland
196. Proctor & Gamble
197. *U.S. News & World Report*
198. Survey Research Center, University of Maryland
199. *The New York Times*
200. Sexuality Research Program, SUNY at Albany
201. Same
202. *Cosmopolitan*
203. National Opinion Research Center (NORC)
204. Same
205. *Esquire*
206. Dr. William H. Frey (Director, Ramsey Dry Eye and Tear Research Center)
207. Same
208. The HUMOR Project (Sagamore Institute, Saratoga Springs, NY)

INDEX

Adult education classes,
15
Airplanes, 177–79
Alcohol, 56, 58–61
Amusement parks, 37
Animal parks, 35
Apples, 78–79
Automated tellers,
145
Automobiles, 170–74,
180–82

Bathroom, 118
Batteries, 188
Beverages, 57, 62, 64
See also Alcohol,
Coffee
Bicycles, 175
Birthdays/Birthday
presents, 3–5
Blood/Blood pressure,
109–10
Bodily functions, 131,
133–36
Books, 28–29
Bowling, 41
Broadway shows, 33
Brownies, 81

Cameras/Photography,
158–59
Camping, 38
Candy, 83
See also specific kinds
Cans/Bottles, 184
Catalogs.
See Shopping/Malls
Censuses, 7
Cereal, 67
Charity, 163
Checks/Credits, 143–44, 146
Cheese, 69
Cleaning, house, 195
Clothing, 152–57, 196
Coffee, 63, 149
Commercials/
Advertising, 16, 18–22
See also Junk mail
Commuting, 14
Cookies, 80
Coupons, 148
Crackers, 68
Crime, 48–49
Crying, 206–7

Dentists/Toothcare, 95–
98, 123–25

INDEX

Diapers, 190
Doctors.
 See Medicine/Medical
  exams
Donuts, 90
Drainpipe openers, 150

Eggs, 66

Fairs/Expositions, 36
Fantasies, sexual, 200–
  201
Federal recreation areas, 38
Fingernails/Toenails,
  126–27
Fish, 72
Flowers, 168
Food, 51, 54–56, 65, 88, 147
 See also Snack food;
  specific kinds
Fruit, 77
 See also Apples
Furniture, 194

Garbage, 185–87
Gifts, 167

Girl Scout cookies, 162
Greeting cards, 5
Grooming.
 See Washing

Hair, 122, 128–30
Hamburgers, 74
Heartburn, 89
Hershey's Kisses, 91
Home improvements,
  192
Hospitalization/Injuries,
  112–15
Hot dogs, 74

Ice cream, 82
Illness, 99–101
 See also Medicine/
  Medical exams
Indoors, time spent, 116

Jobs/Working, 11–14
Junk food.
 See Snack food;
  specific kinds
Junk mail, 23–25

INDEX

Laughter, 208
Laundry, 196
Libraries, 30
Lines, waiting in, 117
Lottery, 161
Love, 202

M&M's, 93
Magazines, 26–27
Meals, eating and
    preparing, 50, 52–53
Meat, red, 70
Medicine/Medical exams,
    102–8, 111, 149–50
Misplaced items, looking
    for, 197
Motor vehicle accidents.
    See Hospitalization/
    Injuries
Movies/Movie theaters,
    32, 42
Moving, 192
Museums, 32
Music, 43

Newspapers, 19
New Year, "ringing in," 6

Operas, 33
Outdoors, time spent,
    116

Parking meters, 139
Pasta, 73
Peanuts, 85
Perfumes, 151
Pies, 79
Plastic, 189
Popcorn, 86
Potato chips, 87
Poultry, 71
Public opinion, research
    and surveys, 47

Radio, 18, 160
Reading materials, 28,
    31
    See also Books;
    Magazines;
    Newspapers
Refrigerator, opening
    door of, 191
Relaxing, 195
Restaurants, 52–53

INDEX

Sex, 203–5

School, 16

Shopping/Malls, 137–38,
140–42

Sleeping, 198–99

Smoking, 132

Snack food, 84
See also specific kinds

Speaking, 45

Spices, 75

Sports
attendence, 34
playing, 136

Sugar, 94

Symphony concerts, 33

Taxes, 8–9

Telephone/Phone calls,
44–46, 160

Television, 16–17, 31, 160

Tootsie Rolls, 92

Toys/Games, 163–66

Transportation.
See specific kinds

Vacations/Trips, 169–71,
177

Vegetables, 79

Vending machines, 55

Vitamins, 87

Walking, 176

Washing/Grooming, 119,
121
See also Hair

Water, 183

Weddings, 40

Weight, 120

Work force, time in, 10

Zoos.
See Animal parks

ABOUT THE AUTHOR

Thomas N. Heymann is the author of *On An Average Day . . .*, *On An Average Day In The Soviet Union . . .*, and *The Unofficial U.S. Census*, all published by Fawcett Books. In addition to his work as a "people's demographer," Thomas N. Heymann is a marketing consultant and a producer of educational media. He holds a Bachelor of Science degree in Radio, Television, and Film from Northwestern University and an MBA in Marketing from Columbia University. He currently resides in Chappaqua, New York, with his wife Grace, son Gabriel, daughter Laura, and Labrador retrievers Allie and Grizzly.